SIMPLE FRAMES

"So it shall be that Men scorch Earth, poison Water, spoil Air, and corrupt Fire. But Four shall be One; as One Heart Ground will give birth to green, Water run sweet, Wind carry new breath, and Flame burn clean. The families of Men will nurture the company of Plants, Stones, Animals, and come with devotion to their Sacred Home."

-The Dream Merlin: Druidic Verses.
Song of The Endtimes, v. 17

SIMPLE FRAMES

Poems of the Four Elements

By
Noel Hewitt Tendick

Laughing Coyote Press
2004

Illustrations by   Kalin McGraw
Author Photo by   Tim Tendick

Visit online for book orders
and other services at   www.deepbluedream.org

Email the author at   bluesky@deepbluedream.org
Email the illustrator at   kalin@artisticmangoes.com

ISBN 0-9740150-1-6

First Edition.
Printed on Recycled Paper

Laughing Coyote Press
www.laughincoyote.com

Dedication

Cheryl Braginsky,
for instilling the love of words,
and modeling a life of devotion to creative expression.

Joyce Raddatz,
a teacher who protected nascent growth
from getting trampled,
and always provided abundant light and water.

Contents

Fire

Water

Acknowledgments

Everyone who has ever touched my life in ways subtle or indelible has a place in this work. However, to specify certain direct assistance in gathering and polishing this collection, I gratefully acknowledge the editorial excellence of Ryan Newton(level supreme), Dan Greenspan, Linda Holiday, Liah Howard, and Aimee Von Bokel.

Thanks to Chandra Agave Llewellyn for the collaboration that birthed *Road Words*; Greg Gordon, for the publishing aid; Tim Tendick and Alicia Livingston for the photo shoots; and Virginia Tendick for the lifetime of vital support. I'm thankful for the gorgeous artwork and copious layout assistance of Kalin McGraw; and for the marvelous website construction by her husband Robert Knight.

Finally, my appreciation to the community of North Bay Aikido, my dear family and friends, and all the players in this great production of Life on Earth.

Foreword

Friends ask me how I can justify killing trees for my book when I claim to be an environmentalist. And the answer is I can't. I can no more justify the consumption of resources for this book than I can justify the clothes that I wear, the food that I eat, the vehicle that I drive, or any of it. On the physical plane, I'm pretty well locked into this materialist culture. Spiritually however, I see a different world. This book is a little step towards Praxis, the place where there is no divorce between my ideals and my daily life.

I make this book an offering, that the song of my heart, it's dreams and hurts, might contribute in some small and utterly mysterious way to the reunification with our radiant selves, and this incredible world. What an amazing time when the illusion of separation fades and we remember everything is drawn from the same Source.

This is a collection of poetry that spans many years and many locales, mountaintops and lonely coasts, college days and quiet practices. This is a collection that's been waiting in notebooks for the chance to catch light and reflect some understanding of the world, if not with answers, at least with questions. It has grown from a light idea to an urgent necessity, not to save the world, but to save my world.

I don't know why I write poetry, why cats bathe themselves and dogs roll in crap, or why the moon creates such delightful chaotic devotion. Rilke asked the young poet to consider whether writing was a matter of life or death to him. I've come to discover, for me, it is. I write poetry because I have to. And it happens to be that I love this world, I love its plant and animal and mineral inhabitants, so that's who I dedicate this to.

I really can't take credit for what you find here. I just happened to stumble along, perceive something amazing, and rest a pen against a page. The rest is beyond my understanding. That's why I have tried to be gentle in the gathering, for a line which makes no sense to me was perhaps sent just for you. All these are for you, just as they're for the elements and the Exquisite within the forms of this world.

That is why they were not content to sit inside a journal. Their clamoring began to keep me up at night, demanding to be shared. So much has been given to me, I feel it a humble and sacred duty to return what I can to the Stream. You know what a joy it is to share your light in the blessedly unique way that's you; how the real purpose lies there, not in what you take.

Silence is a vital space for understanding. When the steady din of narrative subsides, and you step into the stillness, new potentials are suddenly gleaming. What was so real, so fixed, bends into beautiful asanas and connects us to everything.

That said, I highly encourage you to read these poems out loud. Your voice has incredible power, signifying your very own wavelength. When you enter that vibratory realm, it's a whole other category of magic. Words can be tasted in the mind, but they're more enjoyable on the tongue. Whatever the meaning of the work, I hope it holds some meaning for you. Thanks for sharing this space and light with me.

Yours in love and service,
Noel Hewitt Tendick,
aka Reverend Blue Sky

Earth

"Return me to Earth,
that it show me the joy
of this humanbeing,
what it means to infuse body,
occupy space,
feel the world through roots in the ground."

PRAYER OF RETURN

With the flow we open up to the world
and everything is okay,
everything is awake alive and happening
and this is but a passing dream,
a delight, a touch, a letting go
for the spiral of all things great and meaningless.
Allow beauty to move through us,
for its value is not in being held
but in being offered up.
Bless this gift,
not for the redemption of sins,
but for the simple sake of sacrifice.

We are trapped in a grey afternoon
by a sky we cannot see and an earth we do not feel.
We are bound by the love
that rests in the center of hearts,
a sweet solution awaiting the alchemical release,
waiting the spark that sets wings aflame
and puts words in breath.
We listen for new growth,
the green seeds pushing through earth.
Yin nourishes roots and holds them in dark mystery;
Yang feeds us light, draws leaf and stem into the air.
Today we are alive,
thank you Creation, we are alive.
We unfold,
polishing new ways of standing.
We chip and flake,
cut away the old and ungainly,
spin and shape the soft clay.
All because, like the seed,
we drive towards earth and towards heaven.
We desire to be held
and to stand up proudly in the brightness of the world.

Let us be patient in these processes,
let us take the time to inch by determined inch
into that which first gave us life.
Let us know that we are never alone in these seasons,
the nascent spring and bright summer,
the ripe autumn and still winter.
Let us move with grace into light,
arching and swaying in a breeze that moves across all things,
stirring the Exquisite within.

LET EYES LEAVE INK

Beyond the ancient hall of page-bearing oak,
the moon chases shadows
of feather hunting fur.

Offerings left on altars of rain
abandon form
to feed hungry ghosts
and sleeping roots.

Parcels of dream
that have contented themselves
in solitude
carefully mix their elixirs.

The mountain pass
reveals paths of migration,
trails for running on bone
for the agony of wing.

TENCHINAGE*

I lay out on the roof of the world
and all its troubles rest with me.
The moon is a pendulum of light
that crushes physicality.
There is too much loss to heal;
suffering eases into the river.
I give in to all the ruin we've built
with hands of loss,
all the beauty we've ground into dust.
Slender cords keep me here.

I cannot translate the language
spoken at the edge of the world.
It's too agonizing and too beautiful
to pass through into words.

On the verge of stepping off,
a bit of clarity comes.
In scouring this human
with the grim perception of extinction,
the vessel is being cleansed.
Sharp edges are being smoothed,
recesses brightened,
the weight of the world lightened.

On shards of glass I kneel to pray.
I allow my heart its breaking open
and universe to pass through me.
I give myself to the work of the world;
I cast my lot with creation.

*Heaven and Earth Throw

AS WELL AS I CAN

Sometimes
I take the insect life
because it painfully reminds me
of my skin.

Sometimes
I dream the worst in you
because when I was young
my world
blew apart.

Sometimes
I sit in a prison of my own making
without understanding
how to free
myself.

Sometimes,
when the night sky
rips open my chest
and the ground
swallows me whole,
I'm frightened
by how much I love you
and this incredible world.

LIVING QUIETLY INSANE

It seems
in the cultivation of various arts of living,
one generally gathers
a greater sensitivity and awareness
of not only the self
but the surroundings
which one inhabits.
How on earth
can I possibly handle that?

I mean, how can I possibly
face the ruin of a planet
with the calm demeanor
necessary to navigate the frozen foods aisle?

Can you imagine if you were trying to choose
a TV dinner and found some fellow
bawling his eyes out
because over and over and over
we eradicate entire ways of life?

Can you imagine if we actually felt
what extincting just one species
actually means?

How would board meetings run
if they opened with a firsthand understanding of
the devastation of ecosystems
for the profit of a few money-bloated assholes?

Thank god
we have poignant statistics
that don't mean a thing
when we pass our days

without ever touching the ground,
that stir our hearts until we change the channel.

Thank god
the news keeps us
in a constant state of terror and consumption
as the new world order
builds a wall through the yard.

Because when I'm feeling this sensitive -
and really, what would the checkout magazines
think of a man crying like this -
I feel like I can't even get up in the morning

because every step I take
will be seated in the alienation
of a species gone mad.

Sooner or later I do get up
and go to the grocery store.
I hold it together long enough
to buy some boxed degradation
all the while wondering
how are we going to wake up from this nightmare?
What can I do today so our children
won't hate us as much tomorrow?

And I wish that my quiet practices
and my love were enough.

SHADES OF MOVEMENT

I begin to run in clearing fog,
        in a sun-boldened tread that doesn't yet burn.

        I converse with heartbeat,
        sing in sweat,
                pound out a rhythm of leather-
mediated
        flesh on stone.

I count my companions
in fox, vulture, deer;
the bumblebee who pauses
for a bath on my arm.

What else is there?

I would not forget you raven,
nor the wide-open spaces
        that cry in their silence.

The run will be gone soon,
and then there will only be
shades of movement

textured with hoof and paw print,
        currents disappearing into grass.

EVENSONG

I thought I'd be making love
by now,
in a spot in the garden
between pear and plum trees,
next to rows
of incredible vegetables
conferencing their growth
with moonlight.

Can you believe
I passed up the opportunity
to be an otter this afternoon
because the surge of the sea
didn't match

the sinusoidal oscillations
I had charted
on my graph paper?

What am I even doing using
graph paper?

What am I doing trying to get a job
when I spent my childhood years
attending middle class boot camp?

The only thing
I can do about that now
is to keep planting living things,
doing my best to nurture what comes forth
in its tender green.

So as I lie here, waiting for you,
I'll listen in on the evensong
of a different respiration,
a quiet growth in dark places.

What I hear reminds me
that we do have memory
older than thought,
we do have a chance
for an authentic life,
and I am not so sorry
that I am human.

LEAVE IT BE

Have you ever really looked
at the life of a tree?

Have you held the small casing
that sends up
this great being?
Do you see how
it marks experience in rings?
Do you feel roots
underneath you anchoring and drawing up
its very existence?
Do you hear it growing
in every leaf,
singing the greensong
in sunlight and wind?
Do you realize how much
it gives in its natural fall?

Have you learned to speak its language?
Would you ever consider expressing anything
towards it
but gratitude and awe?

AT SACRED GROUNDS

Would you like anything else? you ask.

To extend the bridge of our passing
into a sky of silence looking into light.
To ask nothing of you -
no touch, no sight, no sound -
but simply to be two moments of being;

two collections of space and wind
celebrating the sublimation
of experience
from earth into breath.

No thanks, I say.

And then there is only the leaving.

But your smile was alchemical
and my world is infinitesimally, incredibly changed.

All these droplets,
embodied or leaping,
offer their ripples to river.

They cut and carry grains of rock
and everything changes forever.

SHIN KOKYU

When a great force
      crashes into you,
               your heels
               grow roots,
you sit
in your sacrum
      and turn in the sun
            of this devotional orbit.

        When voices chant in a circle

there is an arrival
             and then nothing but prayer,

like being underwater,

        knowing you really are
           the center of the universe.

FALL SEVEN TIMES, GET UP EIGHT

If you told me what time it is,
I'd be tired.

If I noticed we were balanced
between heaven and earth,
I'd fall.

If someone shouted
and woke up my mind,
I'd find all sorts of things
to worry about getting done
while we sit here,
diligently doing nothing.

> You call this love, all this
> falling and rolling and
> rising again?

BEARING WITNESS

As we moved among
the garden beds,
tending fingers of earth,
oceans in the sky
gathered together,
giving greater obeisance to sun.

We worked through the blue mood
of the cloud-covered evening,
          turning compost,
losing light.

We cut kale, pulled beets,
brought them
and the day of clouds
into the kitchen.

Leaves and roots
steamed and baked,
served in hand-thrown bowls.

We ate at a table
bordered by stone,
          traced grooves worn smooth
          beneath trailing fingertips
and the resignation of eyes
dreaming distant
candlelight.

Conversation clattered on countertops,
so we sat with our thoughts
and our cups of tea
and let night
come.

IN DARKNESS

The pregnant moon
hangs above the hills.

> Do you feel
>> how much power there is
>> in silver?

> Do you realize that the switch you flip
>> means the dammed-river-death of spawning
>> salmon,
>> the coal-smoke-suffocation of communities,
>> the fission-creation of millennial poisons?

Come outside with me tonight.

> I've cleared the path to the garden.

>> It's not often we get to watch the plants
>> sleeping
>>> and the stars turning overhead.

>>> As we sit out on the rise,
>>> the belly of moon
>>> offers us
>>> a moment of grace.

UNBENDING INTENT

This morning you chose
to open your eyes, you chose
your ablution, costume, and consumption.

You felt the planetary alignment,
checked geothermal currents,
received cosmological bulletins

within the space of a breath.

So what are you going to do with it all?
What's the spell you ache to cast
with your magic bean?

It's time to remember.

It's communion with yourself
in divinity's cup;
it's a coven of one.

The moon perfects its course,
waxing praxis.
All the world
partners itself to your prayer.

Cultivate stillness and
nurture this precious seed.

Your power waits to come through you,
it's just a simple choice.

Air

"Return me to Air,
the spirit that eases forth
with whisper above silence,
reflected in eyes shining clear.
Let me open to its touch
and be carried into spaces
beyond understanding."

AWAKEN ONE GIFT

The sudden glimpse of rapture,
the golden drop of dew tasted on
parted lips;
despite the stance of rocks breaking
silence into rapids,
the river reaches the sea.

What dream forms this
mystery working through the gift of clay?
What mind grapples with orbiting moon
while body lies in sunlight,
enticed with its warmth?
Noisy waters, distant wind, the hills of madrone
and meadow bearing benevolent
green into blue, all stillness and expectation:

everything born of perfection
comes to fruition in the wink of the vulture's eye.

I am nothing: I am the sound of remorse,
I am the fall of rain that ends
in mute earth. I am gone.

I am everything: I am wind in crow's
wing, I am the aged oak and the acorn,
I am the cloud-gathering storm.
I open heart and lips to the taste of unceasing life,
I bow to worship at the font of universal knowing:
this gift, this kiss, this solitude.

Spirit of my heart, guide me in your truth.
Teach me forgiveness of the chains that
bind me from this world.
Teach me surrender that I might fall
and learn flight,
teach me how to embrace the love
that waits to come through me.

All to be honored and held,
all to be blessed and let go.

HUMBLED OF REGRET

Early pink reflected in the windows of buses
   trundling home to night. I excuse
myself from the fury of wheels
  for the sake of walking,
   sandled steps in a stilling place
  breaking open the boundaries of self.
I give thanks with hushed jubilation,
obeisance to the first planet-star
  in fading blue, warm with clouds to capitulate
the promise of ocean and footprints
  above the kiss of surf.
I remember tomorrow
   born of action and the power of intent,
I am understanding strength
   by gentleness.

There will be no moon tonight -
  I am left to starlight and the turn
to dark nurturing.
The dead snake has been taken from the
   roadside by unseen paws,
  leaving me to mourn my misgiving
   as the reptile finds new life in mammal.
I do not know the animal that rustles in oak leaves,
nor by what miracle comes the drowsing breath within me,
   so I dissolve small ego for the absolution of dew
and the grace of the Milky Way.
Who am I to close my eyes to this? And yet
  sleep comes.

It is nothing less than the sunrise
  that finds me corporeal once more.

A flight of geese high in the dawn
   reflects the beginning of light.

ONCE MORE AROUND

My room is on the second floor
of the farmhouse,
so that makes the little spider
rappelling outside my window a million miles up
the most courageous little bastard
I've met since not getting out of bed
this morning.

He's framed by a grey sky
and the diffusion of one perception
into another.

Just when I thought he was getting
some good lines set,
he's gone,
and I'm not sure what to do
with myself.

I think I'll allow the wavelength of my body
to choose its own awakening.

THE REINCARNATION OF NEWTON'S APPLE

In my coastal home,
the summer days usually don't have
the searing heat
that scoops water into the sky
and piles up thunderheads
that crash and rend
and spill their waterfalls
onto the ground.

Last night, however, lightning was
startling the patches of clouds,
clashes both sharp and ubiquitous.
Having stopped at different spots
on the ride home to hoot for the shooting
sheets of light,
I at last pulled up a chair on the
back porch.
I just sat,
feeling the scattered thunder rumble
in my chest, letting the currents of
light rattle and soothe me.
I reclined and watched so long it
began to seem as if I had fallen
into my mind,
watching nerve impulses
streak across the crown of my skull.

All the sky my mind alive,
projecting its electricity
in waves and veins,
I began to worry that if I opened
my mouth
the heavens would shoot
right into my belly
and burst my small self.

Teeth bared to bite the lightning,
an apple chose to fall from
the nearby tree
at the next flash.

A noble but not necessarily
noteworthy event,
against the backdrop of storm,
sound magnified by darkness,
it was a deed of great triumph.

That very apple,
filled with sunlight and dirt,
satisfied with height
and having grown tightly into its skin,
chose a midnight fall into blackness,
an uncertain course crashing through
branches and leaves
before bouncing once on the ground
and lying still.

Had it been filled with striving and desire,
it would have waited until I walked
beneath on my way to water the tomatoes,
thus guaranteeing as it fell on my head
a transfusion into mobile meat
and a limited immortality.

But it offered its fall to night,
its wind howling into the abyss.

It crashed and came to rest
under a sky
of lightning and stars.

FULL MOON MISOGI*

To gather the ki of moonlight,
      you must be wearing shoes of grass,
you must row the boat of the gods
      and inhale the sleeping earth.

To digest the ki of moonlight,
      you must remember your tail like a root,
you must love the aspiration of heaven,
      you must have dirt, or the memory of it, under your
fingernails.

To utilize the ki of moonlight,
      you must know how to fall,
you must be open to what you fear,
      you must love the dark, silent places
like you love yourself,
      like you love the world.

*Shinto purification

DID YOU HEAR SOMETHING

The night's gathering
was a certain kind of rapture -
a circle of devotees
reflecting light from the ocean
that was reflecting light from the moon that was
reflecting light from the sun
and around again.

But so many lovelies
with so much love
and so little nudity,
especially while throwing
the frisbee,
made me crazy.

So I traipsed back to the farm,
chanted Kirtan
and put some plants in the ground.

Coyotes yipped,
the moon kept on truckin' through heaven,
and though I gleefully chased shadows
around the garden

I couldn't see
what I was doing,
what regions of darkness
held claws
and which were the understories
of plum trees.

So I went to my sleep
in that peculiar state of grace
that comes from
great enthusiasm and little understanding.

And when I awoke
everything
looked
gorgeous.

PAPER WASP SUTRA

Yesterday, armored, we smoked the Paper Wasps out
with burning frankincense
and ripped their nests from the
bathroom, vents, cupboards.
(Having allowed one family to stay,
they invited their relatives to move in.)
Today they buzz about, non-aggressive
but near frantic.
We prayed to Wasp Spirits,
telling them it was nothing personal, just an issue of space.
We asked them to find a new home,
perhaps a deluxe pine,
shaded, with a view.
We lined the uprooted papier mache
domiciles along the porch
so they could be claimed, maybe even
carried off and re-attached?
The wasps ignored them,
banging themselves silly
against the window.
All the intricacy of
forming a nest layer
by tissue-thin layer,
brushed away like sand.
Now they must surrender their lost pupa
and begin it all over again
somewhere else.
I wonder, do they possess Buddha nature?

SIMPLE FRAMES

Don't think, just write.
You don't need to understand.

You don't need to assemble a
prefabricated dream home
in exquisitely original detail,

complete with beautiful spouse
and perfectly articulated epiphany.

      It's just a poem.

It's a moment
to choose your tools

and study the union of materials
you've gathered.

Feel memory
in the strength of muscle,
survey the blueprint in stillness.

The less you do the better.

Today
you're working in windows,   that's it.

      Simple frames
      to let the light through.

IN COMMUNICADO

What a courageous act to open your
mouth without having decided
what will come out!

There's a certain cosmology
at work here
that we've largely
forgotten,
and when we suddenly
        open the door
                we find not a room
                        but the image's passing
                                through.

                How outrageous to trust the outrageous!
                                Really, who would ask such a
thing,
                        besides
                        the very one
                        who wants
                        to speak.

THE CHARMED UNDERGROUND

What inspiration is there at this hour?
The weight of day's living
solidifies at the bottom of the pan,
residue of incomplete interactions
staining the rim,
a bit of burnt sentiment,
a portion of remorse drying out for
morning disposal.
The company of dreams
waits, watches,
smirks behind masked faces.
Despite immersion in closed carpeted spaces
that ridiculed daylight with fluorescence,
tonight is magic.
Untouchable awakening
in the in-between
renews contact
with wondrous otherworldlies.
We may not have heard their secrets
below neon buzzing,
but our lips
carried their whispered charms.
And tonight the slip of sleep
opens the door
to such wonderful winged chaoses
that even in the morning's fading memory
they will sustain
another day.

REMEMBERING PRAYER

Blessed be this dawning,
       praise and exultation.
Spirit, let me dance as the child dances,
       feet in Earth,
       eyes open to magic.

Blessed be this day,
       journey and discovery.
Spirit, teach me the mystery of creation
       opening in spiral and light.

Blessed be this evening,
       turning round to rest.
Spirit, guide my steps into darkness,
       strengthen weary heart,
       empty heavy hands.

Blessed be this night,
       perfecting stillness.
Spirit, forgive what I am and what I could not be.
       All things sacred and undone,
       ash and breath,
       starlight and bone.

DRAWN INTO SKY

Wind rises under midnight sun,
howls ice off glacier,
abandons desert in curtains of sand.
Teases clouds from specters into feathers,
breaks ocean into white-caps
and mends them into blue.

Eases into forest,
speaking through branches.
Comes low to caress grasses
and the face of a woman
in a meadow,
who lays down
to sleep
in the snowfall
of this beginning.

In morning she
awoke with thin light,
felt the end of storm.
Cold lay over everything,
gentle as white.
She had dreamt of her
old home,
the field where she lay
surrounded by trees
and listened for
the voice of snow.

THE LOST COAST

The trail switches back and forth
to bring me bearing pack
a thousand feet down to shore.
It stretches out through
fields where elk browse,
crosses stream and bends
around the bay.

Feet freed of boots
burrow into black sand
as I watch the sun set beyond
the curve of sea.

Tonight I only need simple things.
Ginger root simmered on stove.
Gibbous moon high over water.
Warm breeze bringing the sound of waves.

A candle, pen, and page.

The candlelight is crucial.
Balanced between wind
and stillness,
the flame wraps its wick,
hurries to glass frame,
worries at the rising pond of wax.
Without its glow, ink waits
behind the gate
while words swim below
articulation in some half-dreamt
imagining.

Sipping tea,
I listen for the words
in escaping tide
and the dreams of elk.
I transcribe the evening
as best I can
until the wind finally rises
and takes the flame.

Now it's just starlight
and a bed of sand.

Fire

"Return me to Fire,
that it purify and clothe me in flame.
Let it burn away the dry and brittle,
let it feed and release
my dancing heart."

POURED OUT

Today we celebrate
the return of bees,
bustling about jasmine and rose.
Today we feel
new sun on skin
and life emerging.
In this fire,
everything burns clear.
Bless old wounds
with your tears -
how quickly they dry,
unless kissed from cheek,
and then they are made communion.
Let us remember the pact of sorrow
rooted in winter,
our cold ritual of loss,
and forgive the hurt
cupped in hands like wine.
Snow returns to motion,
green gives birth to color,
and everywhere the bees
busy themselves with spring.

QUIET LESSONS OF HURRICANES AND HONEYBEES

This morning I ate my breakfast
in the backyard.

    I held a bowl of granola,
    the fog blowing in thin,
    and my body's illness:

        these things offered themselves to the day
        complicit
        and charged with choice.

Rivers sculpted mountains,
bones became blood,
every cell turned over.

            Yet a concentration of conditioning
               maintained its vigilance,

loathe to surrender
its fort of understanding.

The morning overflowed
with morning.

It was enough work to know
just a sliver
    and when a busy mind had its way,

I didn't even notice that.

So I drank my tea
and sat with the smile of wisteria,
    slow creeping shade touching toes
    and the loss of friends.

I felt them all the best I could

and let them go
along the sun's meridian.

STALKING METAPHORS

                    Let me turn my vision to sleep.
Some of the work
already rests here,

sifts through rustling leaves,
rides coyote yelp
and the wind
of invisible wings;
          it moves the pen of its own accord,
          reordering itself in ink.

Some of the work
must be hunted
          across fields of imagination.
It is the poetry of dream
that flees with waking,
hides itself from light.

To chase it you must run
blindly without stumbling.

To capture it
you must crouch
until it comes
to you.

The roosters crow from the old stump,
the morning star is alone
above the orange horizon,
          and I have not slept
          to watch the dance
behind
my eyelids.

Black thins to blue,
      the sun touches treetops,

      bends low to brush my forehead
      where night kissed me good-bye.

DON'T JUST DO SOMETHING, SIT THERE

I'm getting the feeling again
of watching a movie
as I sit on the avenue
drinking tea.

I've lost my zest for movement
or even delightful stillness,
my body resting
as if darkened and slightly reclined.

And the problem is,
I'm not even interested in the show.
Somewhere between junior high
and a long time ago
I lost interest in this type of flick.

The actors are playing their roles
enthusiastically enough,
but I don't see much character development,
the plot's not moving,
and I've heard the director is a cyborg
bent on world domination.

Perhaps I'll find someone
to make out with.

THE DANCE IS FERTILE

Confusing observation with action
is a perilous occupation.

For instance, in scholarly days,
I read pages of statistics
on the devastation of ancient forests,
all with corporate sponsorship
like athletic stadiums,
but kept attending class
as cancers spread.

But when I watched one
thousand year old tree cut down,
cut up,
and dragged away
like a murdered thing,
I locked myself to a bulldozer
with a friend
and stayed there
while loggers yelled and then fell silent
as cops smeared pepper spray
into our eyes.
I allowed them to burn me blind
for the sake of protecting some trees
for a couple of hours.

                        [which were themselves
                        Taken while we sat in jail.]

This is not a soap box confessional;
this is not a badge of self-righteousness.
This is not an alienation of me from you.

This is simply the voice of a guy
who saw some trees fall
and who knelt on a stump and wept.
We hear it all and, whether touched or derisive,
at some level we're torn apart
and somewhere we're all longing
for the harmony that
our stories
remind us is gone.

Since longing doesn't stop chainsaws,
let's stop studying how we're killing our world.
We can protect places green and gorgeous,
build something organic,
love each other with grit and compassion.
So when the beast finally runs out of gas or
blows itself apart,
there will be some space to begin again.

WHEN I POINT AT THE MOON, DON'T LOOK AT MY FINGER

I fast for days
then eat entire plates of potstickers,

was vegan for years
but consume pizza and milkshakes without remorse.

I run races
or go weeks without exercise.

I meditate 11 hours a day,
watch TV 11 hours a day,
sleep 11 hours a day.

I ride my bike to the grocery store in the rain,
I drive 4 blocks to see a movie.

I make love for days
and hold celibacy like an iron bar.

But before every meal I say
Grace:
Let this turn of the hand,
this look, this cherished second,
simply be
all the love that I am.

BECAUSE IT'S ALWAYS BEEN OKAY

When I awoke this morning
I found a note stuck on my forehead
reminding me to stop by the
farmer's market
for broccoli, a samosa, and the
realization of my inherent enlightenment.

I mean really, why the hell not?

ROAD WORDS

On the July stretch of highway
between Colorado and California,
mostly Nevada,
a journal was passed
between two of the occupants
of a pickup truck,
asking some questions.

What color is your desert mind exploring?

"The desert is a view I haven't trusted in too long.
Dry heat saturates my mind with familiarities.
Brown touches my mouth
as red moves up and down my veins warming my chest.
Ocatillo hinted with cholla nectar green penetrates my eyes
and floods my body with each heart beat."
   —Agave

olive pants hanging in heat
become the medium of sweat — blue water long ago
abandoned
turning eyes inward to death's white —
in this desert lies the secret of skull becoming
sand with grace of sun.

What do you find in the desert, what does it find in
you?

I have no need for water.
The desert asks for death — how does one refuse?
The dream of clay falling from crystalline depths.
But wait — my death belongs to ocean,
a pattern of diffusion -
Sorry mojave.
I still love your smile.

"This desert air,
once inhaled,
absorbs water
and questions our liquid beings.
Ocean drips away with each drop of sweat.
At one time your fish scales
fell away and
legs and lungs sprouted
but the mind still in fluid
can be a risk in the hot sun.
As it takes a toll on my writing, my friend."
—Agave

What is your body at the moment?

"I'm a desert tortoise,
hiding in my (camper) shell
from the powerful sun
zooming through this languid land."
—Agave

aching and undone, there are miles untraveled in muscle,
sharp vision
slowly unraveled.

goodness. there's a fury in my gut.
dried apricot and raspberry soda battle
hummus and cabbage.
tortilla and chili have met their own gastro
doom.
should I eat a mint?

Where do you want to be right now? (Besides here)

I want to be a reflection in water,
mirror breaking into a thousand shards
inviting light
to cut and bleed the yearning of one dew drop
to be sea.

I want to stretch
myself between rock and burn the black
of space touching mountain,
with growl and pounce sit zazen in mountain lion gut.
I want to embody
the nonreality of time.

I want to be in the dreams of those who hate me
and terrify them with love.

I want to be in your arms
singing the note that signifies you
explaining you are everything
always loved for it.

I want to be flying across the highway,
smash my brain in the grill of a truck and
be returned to earth with loving hands,
down becoming dust.

I want to be thigh-deep in ocean
with my father's ash upon my brow
as I dive into pulse
and forgive him in depths of slowly swaying kelp.
I want to nap in the core of a comet
casting itself into the sun.

I want to split yinyang,
follow the path of the sun
and the arc of the moon
and crest their respective waves
to find myself again in deep currents,
unwilling to play by gravity's rules.

I want to be in the top of an old growth redwood cut,
and ride it down to thunder.
I want to be in a monastery to
forget I am not a candle
and be blessed by self-immolation.
I want to be in a slot machine and tumble into
one person's brand new life.
I want to be in Iraq to learn what it means
to be American,
in Scotland to disappear into mist.

I want to be in the dance that boils blood to water,
I want to be in the kiss that saves two worlds.
I want to watch the walls come down, the machines all die,
the birth of the universe in infant eye.

"I want to be the rain drops falling on two lovers
purifying Earth."
—Agave

In 500 words or less, describe the differences between biocentrism and deep ecology and what you feel is the most effective approach to steering humanity off the highway to hell. You have 5 minutes. On second thought, what will be your next birth, do you suppose?

Agave takes the fifth.

I am born of a teardrop that reaches chin and falling,
becomes sound.
I am born of howl,
human kneeling naked in moonlight,
wolf that will be poisoned tomorrow.
I am born of fur smashed into asphalt,
harpoon piercing gentle
body song, I am born a child
dying without medicine.

I am born of brother's murdered brother,
suicide and self-destruction,
alcoholism, overdose, battering of the self
because everything is taken away.
I am born of those without home or language
and those that stole them.
I am born
abandoned to the garbage.
I am born of
killers conquerors,
thieves and liars,
yogis priests
gods and goddesses,
sonsabitches and saboteurs.
I am born of you.

I am reborn because the universe demands life.

I am reborn because
I forgot how painful it was last time
and I missed the ache besides.

I am born this moment because there's no other choice —
life is laughing thriving, exultation and flowers,
this life is weeping freezing, mutation and scars.

This life is a dying star
begging light.
To despair and cultivate peace,
to bleed and love in rivulets flowing homeward.
Everything ready and waiting to be born again.

IT COMES TIME TO DREAM

Let's say the entire reason for having a body
is to express love.

That would mean all the gifts your hands
make are love,

and all the miles your feet travel are love,
and all the words you speak
are some form of love.

So I'm going to try this out.

When you strike at me I'll pretend
you're trying to love me in a special way.
I'll welcome it, blend with it,
and show you how much I love you back
by not allowing you to break my face or my heart,
and not trying to break yours.

I'm even going to say there's nothing
wrong with anyone.

I'll be crazy and say we're all drawn from
the same source of perfection,
and just so this doesn't all sound too Santa Cruz,
I'm sitting down, right here,
and letting it all be.

No ears, no eyes, no nose, no mouth,
no past, no future,
just this moment
with entirety
opening in my lap.

        That's getting closer to the heart
        of things.

PASSING THROUGH

Give me your language.
I want a taste of what it means
to be you.

Which lifetime is that smile from?

Whose touch creates your art,
        mends splinters of light into bone?

What name can we give a breath
born in another epoch
that gives us everything we have?

I cannot cradle this moment.

        It is all I can do
        to keep my eyes open
        before the face of forever.

ENOUGH MUMBLING

Man, I drank so much sake last night.
     I love you, man.

Oh I'm sorry, were you asleep?
     It's okay, you know I love you.

Omigod, then my boss caught me checking my email, and
he said -
     I don't care. But I love you.

Onegashimasu!
     Whoa! I love you!

Do you know why I pulled you over?
     I love you?

Do you know where I can score some kind bud?
     No dude, but I love you.

I think it's terrible Dubya didn't get "re"-elected!
     This is a tough one, but I love you.

Como te va?
     Te amo.

It's time for you to start thinking about getting a real job.
     No thanks, but I totally love you.

Can you spare some change?
     I just love you.

Get a job hippie!
     Wahoo, I love you!

Do you want to get together tonight?
     Smokin Moses I love you.

Did you watch Blah Blah on channel Blah last night?
     Hell no. I love you.

Excuse me, where's Ocean Street?
     Boo! I love you.

Yesterday I bought the cutest sweater at The G –
     That's enough. Just know I love you.

Get out of here, I never want to see you again!
     I'm going. I love you.

Meow.
     I especially love you.

               Really people, why the hell not?

AUTUMN COURSES

Autumn courses through me
as a fever,
throbbing in roots,
reddening skin,
making me ache for harvest.

I lie out in the dying days,
air too heavy to move,
sniffing for a hint of rain.
And when the sun
has stopped stuffing me with light,
the cold stroke of night
splits my skin.

I fear the wholesome fall
into metaphor.
Surrender to the vegetable
seems too sweet,
too complete an offering
to passion, consumption, and decay.

So I pluck myself from the branch
and walk toward the mountain's
early winter,
choosing to love a little more carefully
for now.

Water

"Return me to Water,
my ocean soul, tide of immortality.
Teach me release to death's sweet embrace,
teach me to be reborn in these tropical waters.
Teach me the peace of surrender,
letting it all go to find my way home."

BEFORE THE RAIN

Before you speak to me
    of leaves falling
       and the coming rain,

let me look

           at the most beautiful part of

my world

           as I have longed to look,

      with all my heart
        seeing
      through my eyes.

COME TO GROUND

Ask for the blessing
of the elements.

Call down the moon
to guide you through sacred space.
Explore the luscious
blossoming of memory
cleansed of expectations.

Bring me suffering
and I will hold your tear
against the balance of sand.

Where do we find home
in the scattered runes of stone?
Where do we bleed
when dreams turn to ash?

I am not the gatekeeper.

I have watched the sharp rocks
consumed by the sea
at the edge of remembrance.

I have lived in the mandala
of wood and sap
and touched the bellies of gulls in flight.

I have gathered enough wisdom
only to know
the peace in surrender
and the love of freedom.

THE FALL OF LEAVES

Bring the cross,
iron fall
crushing skull heavy with tears
refusing birth.
I ache to bleed.
One whispered word
shakes body,
awakens flight.
This gesture falls defeated.
Universes in the steps
between crouch
and spear,
universes of emptiness
crowd the inches
between eyes
burning closed.
Night of the gentlest misting
perfects body,
soul aches into forgiveness.

Blessed hurt,
undo memory,
summon no ghosts,
let the dead lie.

Sacred moment,
let me honor buried mountains and
the cold, high air.
Ease fists into prayers,
fire into ash,
sky into rain
and be done.

Sweet sleep resolve sorrow.
The last leaf lets go.

PERFECT LONELINESS

I sit and beckon a perfect loneliness,
inviting the words
that, driven from bed to
> beach to yearn beyond the illusion of stars,
> I could not find on my own.
But I'm learning patience.
I'm learning to quiet the mind
and allow poetry to find me
> sitting, back straight,
> > pausing
> for the cat traversing my notebook.
Knowing, in the darkness,
> a love of all beings
and the willingness to express it
in the language I know best.

JEWEL OF REFUGE

Five Brown Pelicans
low into swells
practice kinhin*
in a line of rowing and gliding

until they rise from the cycle
of crests and troughs
to gather cloud
from the aging afternoon.

I watch them
with temple at my back,
standing in the surf
that steals footprints
but leaves feathers,

savoring the stunning cold.

I pretend not to hear the bell
that summons our kinhin,
for it draws me from the ocean
where I want to float,

knowing depths of silence
by my willingness to be silent.

I want to trust in the motion of the sea
that unifies and parts
with the ease of a sphere,
        always whole unto itself.

*Buddhist walking meditation

I watch the pelicans
in noble posture
until they dip

and disappear behind water.

THE TIDE'S BELONGING

I love this wave
arriving with touches of foam
and diamonds trailing down its back.
It raises its face and washes over me.
It lifts
and tumbles
and holds me under its breast,

lets me go on the hard shore
whispering *come with me*
as it disappears.

It's already gone,
part of new waves
rich with the promise of return.

This next wave
will tickle my ankles
and kiss with spray.

The one after
will knock me down,
scrape me under

until I fight my way out
gasping.

It is difficult to trust the waves,
but I love the ocean.

Water is not an easy love
for those who have grown as mountains,

but to learn from the tides,
the constant heartbeat
with ever changing face,
is to learn a perfect love.

KNOW YOUR PLACE

A world strains with expansion.
But the noise of a desperate species
is silenced in the space
of surf and pines
meeting below the cumulus drift.

If you gaze without looking,
there are patterns
on the water's face.

Surrender expectation,
attachment to direction,
for ocean has known better
all along.
Currents move
with moon, wind, and whimsy
through a universe
that marks cause and effect
with grains of sand.
Look not to the everlasting,
the names carved in stone's
slow decay.
Do not name
the forces moving through you.
Accept the honor of the messenger
without knowing
all the ends to which you work.

Look to the reflection of night
in the depth of water.
Understand that
you are lost without hope
in the endless sea,
you are held
and drifting.

Neither time nor
the exaltation of enterprise
matter here.

The humility of your hands,
given shape and set free,
is the fulfillment of your
beginning.

MONTANA'S TWILIGHT

This evening brings rain
thundering on the yurt's canvas roof,
quiet in the field.
It sings softly on mullein leaves,
on my hat.
It trickles rivulets down
my arms,
taking away the work of the day.
I stand and surrender muscle,
this trap of body heat.
I let the rain cool me as it
bends grass,
holding down the dust of the road.

BLUE BELLY

All the world conspires for heat.
Golden hills reflect light,
sky offers no resistance
to sun's sharp messengers
who hit atmosphere
and disperse,
bleaching blue,
blinding eyes.
Skin slicks,
wearing its thin coat of protection,
a countermeasure
nearly useless
in noon-dead air.

In the midst of the slow dissolution
of molecular assemblage,
we find a concrete scoop
wedded to salvation.

The blue belly
welcomes all,
swallowing splash and gasp,
holding the body redefined
by a cold
quite indifferent
to day's heat.

Lying out on the grass,
sun warms
with soft fingers,
brushing away little lakes.
Wind's subtle shifts
arouse skin
and we glide
on new currents.

The clay of our bodies
melts and cools again
in aqueous midwifery,
a luscious cycle
of summer play.

BURDEN OF NIGHT

Cars cut slivers of rain
from the sound of dusk
as they caravan home to port.
Cloud like dragon's beard
breathes across smoke stained cover,
water cleansing sins in backyard confessionals.
Streetlight vigils burn holes
in the thigh of night as it
squeezes earth between its legs.

I have no name for her.
She whispers for me with fierce droplets,
pelting my neck and running down my chest.
She works in rivers,
smoothing away chalk drawings
and bearing newspaper sail boats
to storm drains.
The houses run, oil on canvas.
Everything slips past me
as I stand on the sidewalk.
Her water raises
a dorsal ridge of white fins on my feet.
I do not submit and
she continues her tiny-toothed assault.

The kitchen lights are off now,
the sour yellow halos
of streetlight angels about to implode.
The ripe solidity of earth
tumbling into space
awakens no suburban devotees.
Slumber shields them
from the moment before collapse.

I'm one witness to the pause
between cataclysm
and redemption, sung by gurgling sewer caps.
Time seeds the clouds
the earth holds,
and still, she rains.

OUT THERE

In the greyblack solitude
one heart struggles to be born,
struggles against cage of bone
for the chance to be ash
silent as redtail's flight circling
on currents of gold.

Another begs for memory,
begs and softly steals tears
from the night of mare's tails,
drinks and yields to a voice of distance
that promises one brush of angel wing
for the sake of resurrection.

And here, what is the dream of this tired heart?
Stillness.
Final breath of starlight
as a kiss
soft as lips whispering prayers.

Incense in Poseidon's temple
infuses mist, blanket of stone.
Honor the silence beneath waves,
there to sing one sacred note
and be still.

THE GOLDEN EIGHT

Yesterday I ran on bluffs,
jumped in the ocean,
spoke with exquisite people:
wrote a poem,
did qigong.

Today I slept all morning,
sat under sorrow's weight,
argued with family:
wrote a poem,
did qigong.

Tomorrow's weather is uncertain
and I haven't read
my horoscope:
I'll write a poem
and do qigong.

INEVITABLE ENLIGHTENMENT

Giving up,
I jumped ship
only to learn
the point of that life
was being in water.

FROM THE ONE HEART

What are you still doing here?
The artifice
collapsed
long ago.

We gave up
the pretense
of existing for the world.

It's just us,
no need for explanation or
elaborate articulation.

The truth already
lives
within.

We aren't getting any closer to it
by dancing with words

so let's lie still,
breathe deeply,
and

~Fin~

About the Author

Noel has studied the art of living in Oregon, Montana, Humboldt County, Half Moon Bay, Hawai'i, the Utah Canyonlands, and Santa Cruz, where he currently resides.

He fills his days training in Aikido, riding sinusoidal oscillations, climbing rock walls, practicing massage, and sitting around, among other things.

He is doing his best to soften the concrete view of the present reality in ways other than mashing his head against it.

He's incredibly thankful for his life, and he holds you partially responsible for that.

bluesky@deepbluedream.org

Photo by Tim Tendick

About the Illustrator

Kalin McGraw is a freelance illustrator who lives with her husband, Rob, and menagerie of imagined pets in Santa Cruz, California.

kalin@artisticmangoes.com

Also Available From Laughing Coyote Press

Gringos in the Mist: A Naturalist's Journey Through Ecuador
by Greg Gordon

Presented as a narrative travelogue, Gringos in the Mist tells the story of oil exploration in the Ecuadorian Amazon and describes the efforts by local and indigenous groups to protect the cultural and ecological integrity of the rainforest. Gringos in the Mist also examines the social and environmental implications of tourism and raises fundamental questions regarding our need to travel.

"We hear that indigenous cultures and naturally evolved ecosystems are vanishing at a horrendous rate. Greg Gordon went to South America to see for himself. The story he tells is vividly detailed, often brilliantly said—implying that we must take care, learn to re-imagine what it is we desire—or risk vanishing ourselves. This is an important, heartbreaking, useful book." - William Kittredge

To order send $16.95 to:
Laughing Coyote Press
P.O. Box 571
Gardiner, MT 59030

For more information on this and other titles by Greg Gordon,

Visit www.laughincoyote.com

To order additional copies of *Simple Frames*
and learn more, go to
www.deepbluedream.org